HENRY PURCELL

The Story of his Life and Work

by Imogen Holst

BOOSEY AND HAWKES

NOTE

I am indebted to J. M. Dent and Sons Ltd for permission to quote Purcell's Will and Petition from Sir Jack Westrup's *Purcell*; to Novello and Co Ltd for quotations from *Roger North on Music*, edited by John Wilson; to Mr H. P. Cart de Lafontaine for quotations from *The King's Musick*, by H. C. de Lafontaine; and to the Oxford University Press for extracts from *Henry Purcell: Essays on his Music*, which I have edited.

In quoting from original seventeenth century sources I have reluctantly modernized the spelling, as it takes too long to recognize familiar words when they are as startlingly disguised as Dr Blow's 'Samibreif, Minom, or Chrochet.'

I. H.

The illustrations are reproduced by courtesy of the Trustees of the British Museum

© 1961 by Hawkes & Son (London) Ltd
Printed in Great Britain by the Westerham Press Limited
High Street Westerham Kent

ALTHOUGH Purcell, at the time of his death, was considered 'the Pride and Wonder of the Age', we know very little about the events of his life. We do not even know anything definite about where or when he was born, or who his parents were. There is some doubt as to whether Thomas Purcell was his father and Henry Purcell his uncle, or whether it should be the other way round. His birthplace was probably Westminster, and the date must have been some time in 1659, for the inscription on his memorial tablet in Westminster Abbey tells us that when he died on 21 November 1695 he was in his thirty-seventh year.

In 1659 the eleven years of the Commonwealth were nearly over, and English musicians were looking forward to the Restoration that was to restore the King and bishops and nobles to power. When all the bells of London rang out for the coronation of Charles II in April 1661 the sound must have filled every house in Westminster, and it is just possible that one of Purcell's earliest recollections was of being held up to see the crowds that were waiting for a glimpse of the royal procession. His father and his uncle both took part in the coronation service in Westminster Abbey. Dressed in the scarlet livery of the Gentlemen of the Chapel Royal, they sang in the 'anthems and rare music, with lutes, viols, trumpets and organs'.

Thomas Purcell and the elder Henry Purcell were composers as well as singers and players, and there can have been very few days when the young Henry Purcell was not listening to the sound of a harpsichord or a lute or a violin. Brought up in a musician's home, he must have learnt the language of music just as easily as the language of words.

He had five brothers and two sisters, but we know nothing of their early life together: we can only guess the anxiety in their home during the Great Plague of 1665 which killed so many Londoners, and the upheaval during the Great Fire of 1666 which lasted for five days and destroyed the whole of the old city, from the Temple to the Tower. By the time Purcell went to school a new London had been built in place of the mediaeval city he had known as a small child. A contemporary eye-witness has described the transformation: 'the dreadful effects of the fire were not so strange as the rebuilding of this great city, which by reason of the King's and Parliament's care, and the great wealth and opulency of the city itself, was rebuilded most stately with brick (the greatest part being nothing before but lath and lime) in four or five years' time.' Sir Christopher Wren's design for the new St Paul's Cathedral was in the magnificent Italian style of St Peter's, Rome, and another eye-witness has described 'the multitude of workmen, the bulk of the stones and the prodigious circumference of the pillars' which amazed the citizens who stood watching the builders at work.

In Purcell's time it was only a short walk from Westminster to the open country, where Londoners could listen to the nightingales or smell the new-mown hay. But London itself was already a noisy place to live in. A seventeenth-century poet has written of 'The crowd, the buzz, and murmuring of this great hive, the City'. And a seventeenth-century journalist has described the clamorous street-criers:

> 'Make room there!' says a fellow driving a wheelbarrow. A tinker bawls, 'Have you brass-pot, iron-pot, skillet or frying-pan to mend?' . . . Another yelps, 'Two a groat and four for sixpence, mackerel'. Here a sooty chimney-sweeper takes the wall of a grave alderman, and a broom-man jostles the parson of the parish.

Even Hyde Park was crowded: 'people coached it to take the air, amidst a cloud of dust able to choke a foot-soldier, which hindered all from seeing those that came hither on purpose to show themselves'. The newly-opened coffee-houses were fashionable meeting-places for those who enjoyed 'admirable discourse till 9 at night'. Here Pepys and his friends were able to discuss the latest scientific discoveries of the Royal Society or the latest publications of the poets. Milton had recently finished his *Paradise Lost*. Herrick was still alive, though he was now a very old man. Marvell and Vaughan and Bunyan were still writing, but the poet who attracted the most attention was the young John Dryden. He had been made Poet Laureate in 1668, when he was still in his thirties, and he already had his own special seat in the most fashionable of the coffee-houses.

*   *   *

It was probably in 1669 or 1670 that Purcell was sent to the state-supported choir school of the Chapel Royal in Whitehall. There were twelve children in the school, and we know from the Lord Chamberlain's accounts in the Record Office that the master was paid an annual sum 'for the children's learning on the lute and violin, for fire for the music room, for ruled paper, pens and ink, for strings for the lutes, and for other services'. The pay was seldom enough to cover all the expenses. Since the Restoration everything was 'mightily altered from Cheapness to Dearness'. And, what was worse, the Treasury was often late with its payments. Charles II lived from hand to mouth and was constantly in debt. Pepys, in his diary for 1666, says: 'Many of the music [i.e., the musicians] are ready to starve, they being five years behindhand with their wages'. This sounds like the exaggeration of casual gossip, but the official records bear him out: there is an entry referring to a payment 'to Thomas Purcell for Wages due for four years and three quarters'. In the year before Purcell went to the choir school the master of the Children, Captain Cooke, had had to refuse to let the boys sing in the services until he had been paid what was owing to him.

There had been no music in the Chapel Royal during the years of the Commonwealth, and Captain Cooke must have found it difficult to train inexperienced boys in time for the coronation of Charles II. But when Purcell went to the school there was already a high standard of singing.

Captain Cooke held many auditions before choosing his twelve boys, and he used to travel to cathedrals as far away as Hereford in search of the best voices. The anthems they sang with the grown-ups of the Chapel Royal choir were mostly by the great sixteenth-century English composers such as Byrd and Tallis. This was music that could never sound out-of-date, and there were probably many seventeenth-century listeners who agreed with Thomas Mace of the University of Cambridge that 'in this present Age we nothing at all Excel or Exceed those Divine Works of the never-to-be-forgotten admired rare Authors of the last Century of Years, whose names are recorded in our Church-Books, and (doubtless) will be preserved, as precious Monuments and Examples to all after Generations, so long as the World and the Church endure.' Some of the anthems Purcell sang as a boy were composed by elderly though still active Gentlemen of the Chapel Royal, including the venerable Dr William Child, who had been born in 1606 and who lived to the great age of ninety-one. But several works were by the young composers John Blow and Pelham Humfrey, ex-pupils of Captain Cooke, who were only ten or twelve years older than Purcell himself. They had begun composing while they were still 'Children' at the choir school, and the King had encouraged them. For Charles II, unlike Thomas Mace, was bored by Byrd. We are told by a Chapel Royal choir-man called Tudway that 'His Majesty, who was a brisk and Airy Prince, coming to the Crown in the Flower and vigour of his Age, was soon tired with the Grave and solemn way, and ordered the Composers of his Chapel to add symphonies etc. with Instruments to their Anthems. . . . Some of the forwardest and brightest Children of the Chapel, as Mr Humfrey, Mr Blow, etc., began to be Masters of a faculty in Composing. This his Majesty encouraged by indulging their youthful fancies, so that every month at least, and afterwards oftener, they produced something New of this Kind.'

The King had heard a good deal of modern music during the years when he had been exiled in France. He had seen several of Lully's operas in Paris and had been delighted with the 'airy' dance music he had heard at the court of Louis XIV. Back in Whitehall, he did all that he could to reinstate the French musicians who had been employed before the Commonwealth. And when the young composer Pelham Humfrey showed a keen interest in the new style of instrumental music he sent him to France and Italy for several years, on a royal travelling scholarship. (The Treasury managed to pay the expenses by taking money out of the Secret Service funds.)

Humfrey came back 'an absolute Monsieur' after his foreign travels. He was made a Gentleman of the Chapel Royal, and in 1672, although he was only twenty-five, he was given the post of composer for His Majesty's violins. In that same year Captain Cooke died, and Pelham Humfrey succeeded him as master of the Children. Purcell was thirteen years old, and we can imagine what it meant to him to have composition lessons from a brilliant young musician who had just heard so many exciting first performances in France and Italy. It was not Purcell's first introduction to foreign styles, for Captain Cooke had been a singer 'after the Italian manner'. But Humfrey was able to teach him far more about the new music that was then being written.

*   *   *

The 'new' music of the seventeenth century is sometimes described as 'Baroque', in contrast with the earlier music of the Renaissance. In Renaissance music the voices or instruments are all equally important. The parts are continually interweaving, so that the tune seldom stays for long in the top voice, but is frequently changing about from the bass to one or other of the middle voices. In Baroque music the tune goes to the top, while the bass is content to provide a firm foundation for it. Renaissance

7

tunes move stepwise for most of their time. ('Up and down stairs', as a seventeenth-century writer puts it.) But Baroque tunes, being safely supported from below, can afford to leap up or down in wide, expressive intervals. And they are free to indulge in quick runs and flourishes which would have been impossible in the closely inter-woven part-writing of the Renaissance.

Sixteenth-century composers seldom bothered to say what instrument they wanted on any particular line: they just wrote 'first voice, second voice, third voice, fourth voice, fifth voice', and left it to the performers to divide the music up as they liked among strings and wind instru-ments and singers. This may seem a strange method of composing, but there was nothing casual about it, for the Renaissance music was written in such a way that the balance of parts was sure to sound satisfactory. Baroque composers, however, insisted on having whatever instru-ment they had been writing for. Ever since the earliest experiments in Venice, nearly a hundred years before Pelham Humfrey was teaching Purcell, composers had been listening to the contrasting tone-colours of brass and woodwind and strings, and had used those colours as an essential part of their music.

*　　*　　*

Purcell's exciting lessons did not last very long, for his voice broke when he was fourteen and he had to leave the choir school. But he was able to stay on at the Chapel Royal as apprentice to the keeper of instruments. An entry in the records for June 1673 says: 'Warrant to admit Henry Purcell as [assistant] keeper, maker, mender, repairer and tuner of the regals, organs, virginals, flutes, . . . courtals and all other kinds of wind instruments whatsoever, in ordinary, without fee, to His Majesty.' It was an excellent opportunity of getting practical ex-perience of the instruments he had been learning about in his composition lessons. 'Regals' were small portable

8

organs that could be moved from one room to another. The word 'virginals' is misleading: it was used for harpsichords and spinets, as well as for virginals. 'Flutes' were recorders. The 'other kinds of wind instruments' included the oboe, which was spelt 'hoboy' from the French 'hautbois'. This Baroque oboe was not nearly so shrill and coarse-toned as the mediaeval shawm, which could only be enjoyed when heard out of doors, or in a very large building. The new oboe was gentler in tone, and the leader of Charles II's violinists said that 'with a good reed' it was 'as easy and soft as the recorder'. The 'courtals' that Purcell looked after were small bassoons: a 'double courtal' was a larger, deeper-voiced instrument, but its notes were not as low as those of our modern double bassoon. Purcell must have had a good many trumpets in his care, for there had been seventeen trumpeters playing in the procession on Coronation Day. Their instruments could only produce 'open' notes, which meant that all their tunes were high and bright and piercing. (It was not until the nineteenth century that valves were used in brass instruments, making it possible for players to get any of the low notes they wanted.) The trombones in the Chapel Royal were still called by the mediaeval name 'sackbut', from the French 'sacqueboute', meaning 'pull-push'. They had a rich and mellow tone that was very impressive, and they were only used on solemn occasions.

Purcell obviously worked very hard as an apprentice tuner and repairer, for he was only sixteen when he was appointed organ tuner at Westminster Abbey. The organist, John Blow, had been one of his teachers at the Chapel Royal, and he was to prove a lifelong friend. It was probably from Blow that Purcell had lessons in what we now call 'harmony at the keyboard'. In the British Museum there is a manuscript in Blow's writing that is headed 'Rules for playing of a Through Bass upon Organ or Harpsichord'. 'Through bass' or 'thorough bass' is the

English equivalent of the *basso continuo* of Baroque music. This word 'continuo' is perplexing. There have been several suggestions about its origin: the most convincing explanation is that it began with the Italian organists of the late Renaissance who were asked to play chords throughout long, elaborate works for double chorus. The chords needed the perpetual support of a bass line, but in the interweaving part-writing the voices crossed each other, and the bass singers often had as many as a dozen bars' rest. So the Italian organists followed the actual lowest notes of the music, in whatever voice they occurred, moving from first bass to second tenor, and even up to one of the alto lines if necessary. In this way they made themselves a 'continued bass' throughout the whole length of the music. And to make it easier to pick out the right vertical chords from so many interwoven horizontal lines, they invented a sort of musical shorthand, writing figures against the bass notes to remind them what chord they needed. For instance, the figure $\frac{6}{3}$ told them to play the third and the sixth above the bass. If sharps or flats were needed, they were written at the side of the figure. (The sign for a natural was not used in the sixteenth or seventeenth century, so in Purcell's manuscripts a sharp always means 'a semitone higher', while a flat means 'a semitone lower'.)

This method of figuring a bass was a blessing to the Baroque composers. They needed a keyboard instrument to fill in the missing notes of the chords that were outlined by the supporting bass and the tune. By writing the short-hand figures they could leave it to the harpsichord player to improvise a part that would realize their intentions. The notes of a chord could be spaced in any order above the bass note, and there was no need to play them simultaneously; they could be spread out slowly and expressively, or divided into even quavers, or broken up into cascades of arpeggios, according to the nature of the tune.

* * *

The art of improvising from a figured bass died out in the second half of the eighteenth century, and today there are perhaps fewer than half a dozen harpsichordists in England who can realize a Purcell continuo at first sight, in a manner the composer would have approved of. In 1674, English musicians would have been considered illiterate if they had not been able to sight-read a figured bass, and Blow's young pupils must have been grateful to him for his 'Rules for playing of a Through Bass'. Among these 'Rules' it is interesting to find a written-out example of a cadence that eighteenth- and nineteenth-century writers on music considered 'uncouth' and 'barbarous'. This is the cadence that uses a major seventh together with a minor seventh. Purcell loved the sound of it so much and used it so often in his music that it is sometimes called the 'Purcell cadence'. But it was not a seventeenth-century invention. It was used throughout the sixteenth century by the great English composers of the Renaissance. And we know that Purcell had found it in their works, for he copied out several of their anthems in a large volume dated 1677 to 1682. This volume is now in the Fitzwilliam Museum in Cambridge, and the notes and the words are as clear to read as when they were written. A handwriting expert has recently described Purcell's manuscripts as 'robust' and 'deliberate', with each letter 'full-blown and boldly formed'. 'The writing', he says, 'is plainly the hand of a man who thought clearly and methodically and knew what he was about.' He also mentions that the notes are carefully placed 'so that the reader or performer cannot have the slightest doubt as to Purcell's intentions.'

The sixteenth-century anthems in this manuscript volume give us a vivid glimpse of what was going on in Purcell's mind during his late teens. We know so little about him as a person, but when we turn the pages of this book we know for certain that he was creating for himself the imagined sound of anthems by Byrd, Tallis, Orlando

Gibbons and the other 'never-to-be-forgotten' composers. Several of the anthems may have had a direct influence on his own works: at 'O that I had wings like a dove', in Adrian Batten's *Hear my prayer*, the frequent repetition of the rising phrase 'then would I fly away' is very much in Purcell's way of thinking. And having copied Nathaniel Giles's setting of 'Our eyes have seen our desire', he wrote his own setting of the same words, only three pages further on.

*　　*　　*

The earliest Anthems that Purcell wrote were mostly in the same form as the Renaissance anthems, for four to eight voices. The style, however, was very different. The voices were seldom as independent as in the polyphonic ('many-sounding') sixteenth-century music: they often moved simultaneously in homophonic style, enjoying the expressive intervals of Baroque harmony. These early anthems are called 'full' anthems: they use all the voices all the time. Purcell later wrote 'verse anthems,' which were like what we now call cantatas. One voice would sing a whole verse as a solo, accompanied by a realization of the figured bass on the organ, and the singers in the chorus would sing short sections between the verses, and also the final 'Glory be to the Father', to bring the anthem to an impressive end. On Sundays and important festivals the verse anthems often had introductions and interludes for string orchestra, in the style that Charles II had encouraged in the early years of the Restoration. The string introductions were called 'symphonies'. This title has nothing to do with the full-length works of the late eighteenth or nineteenth century: in Purcell's time the word still kept its original meaning of 'agreeing together in sound'. The string interlude was called a *ritornello*, because it was often in the form of a refrain, with the strings commenting on the music that had just been sung.

There were members of the congregation in the Chapel Royal and Westminster Abbey who disapproved of violins in church: they complained that the sound was 'frivolous', owing to its associations with the latest dance music from Paris. But the great Baroque composers of Europe knew that there was no hard and fast dividing line between sacred and secular music. They refused to listen to those critics who said that there should be one particular style of music suitable for the church. And they filled their symphonies and *ritornelli* with music that was intensely passionate or energetically cheerful, according to the words of the psalm they happened to be setting.

*   *   *

Purcell showed such an understanding of the possibilities of writing for strings that in 1677, when he was only eighteen, he was appointed 'composer in ordinary with fee for the violin to His Majesty'. The appointment was 'in the place of Matthew Locke, deceased'. Locke had been one of Purcell's closest friends. They had probably known each other since the time when Purcell was quite a small child, for an entry in Pepys's diary for February 1660 says: 'I met with Mr Locke and Purcell, [his father or his uncle] and with them to the Coffee House, into a room next the water, by ourselves, where we spent an hour or two [and] had variety of brave Italian and Spanish songs.' Locke was a teacher as well as a composer, and one of his published works tells us that he wrote 'for the Hands, Ears and Patience of young Beginners'. It is just possible that he may have helped Purcell during his schooldays by showing him how to get used to the feel of the keyboard, for in his 'Certain General Rules for Playing upon a Continued-Bass' there is an excellent piece of practical advice for avoiding forbidden consecutives. He says: 'For the prevention of successive Fifths and Eighths in Extreme Parts the certainest way for a beginner is to move his Hands by contraries: That is, when one Hand ascends, let the other descend.' And we know that he took a friendly interest in Purcell's earliest compositions, for there is a letter saying:

> Dear Harry,
> Some of the gentlemen of His Majesty's music will honour my poor lodgings with their company this evening, and I would have you come and join them: bring with thee, Harry, thy last anthem, and also the canon we tried over together at our last meeting.
> Thine in all kindness,
>
> M. Locke.

When Locke died, Purcell wrote an elegy 'on the death of his Worthy Friend', praising him as a composer 'whose skilful harmony Had charms for all the ills that we endure'.

Purcell's new appointment meant that he was responsible for providing the music for the King's band of 'twenty-four violins'. Charles II had ordered this band to be formed when he first came to the throne, in imitation of the 'Vingtquatre violons du Roi' he had heard at the court of Louis XIV. With memories of the splendours of Paris still fresh in his mind, the King ordered that the players should be dressed magnificently: an entry in the records for 1674 mentions a 'warrant to make up habits of several coloured rich taffetas for four and twenty violins, like Indian gowns, with short sleeves to the elbow and trimmed with tinsel about the neck and at the sleeves, and girdles of tinsel after the same manner . . . and four and twenty garlands of several coloured flowers for each of the violins.' The description sounds as if the garlands were meant to be hung round the necks of the instruments, but the word 'violins' refers to the performers. They played all the instruments of the violin family, including the 'tenor violin' (viola) and the 'bass violin' (cello), for the band was the equivalent of our modern string orchestra.

Violins were a recent innovation, and seventeenth-century opinions about them varied from 'a sprightly instrument, much practised of late', to 'a High-Prized Noise – fit to make a man's Ear Glow and fill his brains full of frisks.' The instruments that were previously used were the viols. They had six strings, tuned, like the lute, in perfect fourths with a major third in the middle. The strings were slacker than violin strings, but although the tone was less brilliant it was never muddy, for the gut frets gave the clear sound of an open string to every note. The bows were held with the palm of the hand facing upwards, which meant that even the smallest viols had to be held downwards, resting on or between the knees. For this reason they were described as *da gamba*, 'of the leg', to distinguish the smaller viols from the violins which were *da braccio*, 'of the arm'.

Chamber music enthusiasts in seventeenth-century England kept a 'chest of viols' – a set of six instruments consisting of two trebles, an alto, a tenor and two basses. They played together 'in consort', having a great many pieces for three, four, five or six instruments to choose from. And they kept up their chamber music during the difficult years before the Restoration, for we are told that 'in private society, many chose rather to fiddle at home than to go out and be knocked on the head'. But the fashion began to die out soon after Charles II had announced that he preferred violins 'as being more airy and brisk than viols'. The bass viol, or *viola da gamba*, lasted the longest, and sixty years later Bach was writing three of his greatest sonatas for *viola da gamba* and harpsichord. But even in Purcell's time the 'whole consort of viols' was considered old fashioned, and composers preferred writing for a mixed or 'broken' consort of violins and viols.

*　　*　　*

It was possibly for this mixed consort that Purcell wrote

15

his string fantasias in 1680. In a sudden spurt of excited energy he wrote one after another, adding the date between the first two staves on the paper, so that when we look at the manuscript in the British Museum we can see a fortnight of his life spread out in front of us as we turn the pages and read: 'Fantazia June the 10. Fantazia June the 11. Fantazia June the 14. Fantazia June the 19. Fantazia June the 22. Fantazia June the 23. Fantazia June the 30.' And before the end of the year he had written another six.

In these string works Purcell was following a tradition that had flourished in England for well over a hundred years. The 'Fancy' was described by Thomas Morley in 1597 as 'music made without a ditty; that is, when a musician taketh a point [i.e., a note] at his pleasure, and wresteth and turneth it as he list, making either much or little of it according as shall seem best. And in this may more art be shown than in any other music, because the composer is tied to nothing.' And in 1665 Purcell's contemporary, Christopher Simpson, was agreeing with Morley when he wrote that 'of Music designed for Instruments, the chief and most excellent for Art and Contrivance are Fancies'. In one of Purcell's Fantasias he chooses to make so much of one particular note that he builds a whole piece of music round a persistently-sounding middle C. But in this and the other fantasias there is nothing old-fashioned about the art and contrivance of the part-writing. He shows his obvious delight in the skilled use of Renaissance devices such as close canon, inversion and augmentation, but he brings to the traditional pattern of the music the whole wealth of his individual mind, so that every phrase sounds unmistakably his own. Even in the six- and seven-part *In Nomines*, where he is 'tied' to the plainsong antiphon 'Gloria tibi Trinitas', the writing never sounds like imitation sixteenth-century counterpoint. It is one of the chief glories of Purcell's music that he was able to take just what he wanted from the best of all possible worlds.

Henry Purcell. A drawing attributed to Kneller

Purcell's musical handwriting, from the manuscript of his
Fantasia upon one Note

The dating of the Fantasias gives us a sure knowledge of the music that was in Purcell's mind during that summer of 1680, but we get no such clear idea of what was going on in his everyday life. If he had travelled from one country to another we might have been able to read long, detailed letters describing the people he was with and the things that were happening to him. But the whole of his working life was spent in the Palace of Whitehall or Westminster Abbey, and he can seldom have travelled further than Windsor. We know that he was married in either 1680 or 1681. His wife's Christian name was Frances, but we know nothing else about her. It is possible that her surname was Peters, for one of their children was christened 'Mary Peters', and a 'J. B. Peters' witnessed Purcell's will during his last illness. Nothing is known about Purcell's married life with Frances except that they had six children, four boys and two girls. Their first three sons all died when they were only a few months old. The house where they lived was in St Ann's Lane (now St Ann's Street), Westminster. Purcell was able to afford the upkeep of a home, for he had been appointed organist of Westminster Abbey in 1679, and two years later he was made one of the three organists at the Chapel Royal, in addition to his work at the Abbey.

The Chapel Royal was the more important of the two posts, and Purcell's duties were clearly set out. 'Of the three organists, two shall ever attend; one at the organ, the other in his surplice in the quire, to bear a part in the Psalmody and service. At solemn times they shall all three attend.' There were Matins at 10 and Evensong at 4 on every weekday. The members of the choir, who were known as Gentlemen of the Chapel Royal, had to attend every day, working in shifts, a month at a time. And when the Court moved to Windsor, a certain number of singers had to go with them. (Travelling expenses were seldom provided, so the Gentlemen must have found life difficult at times.)

The full choir consisted of twelve schoolboys singing treble, and thirty-two Gentlemen singing counter-tenor, tenor and bass. The counter-tenors were never asked to sing very high. It seems probable that the counter-tenor voice was more like a light, high tenor than an alto. Tenors and counter-tenors had to be able to change parts if necessary, for there are entries in the records which mention several singers who were 'to be sworn into the next place of a lay tenor or counter-tenor', or 'to come into pay when the next tenor or counter-tenor's place shall be void'. There is a traditional belief that Purcell was a counter-tenor. This is owing to a music critic's remark in *The Gentleman's Journal* after the first performance of one of Purcell's greatest works, where mention is made of the 'universal applause' that greeted a difficult and elaborate counter-tenor solo sung 'by Mr Purcell himself'. This is the only existing reference to Purcell's singing, and if he had really been such an outstanding performer it seems unlikely that we should not have heard more about his voice. One of the present music critics of *The Times* has put forward an ingenious suggestion. He points out that Purcell's autograph score of the work has the name of Mr Pate, a well-known counter-tenor, written against the beginning of this song, and he asks, with a journalist's fellow-feeling of sympathy, 'could someone have scribbled down 'Mr P.' in his notes and misinterpreted them when he came to write the occasion up?' The only scrap of authentic evidence we have about Purcell as a singer is a choir list proving that at any rate on one occasion he walked in procession with the basses when he was not on duty at the organ.

Purcell's bass parts make considerable demands on his singers. The compass often reaches two octaves, and sometimes extends beyond it. In twentieth-century performances of his music it is quite usual for chorus basses and baritones to have to work in partnership, the one taking over from the other as soon as the part goes too high or too low.

The name 'Gostling' appears in Purcell's own writing against some of the most difficult bass solos in his works. This was the Reverend John Gostling, 'that stupendous bass', who sang in the Chapel Royal for over fifty years. He was famous for his low notes, and Purcell had already begun writing solos for him before he had been appointed organist at the Chapel.

* * *

It was in 1683 that Purcell's first published work appeared. The title page reads: 'SONATAS OF III PARTS: TWO VIOLINS And BASS: To the Organ or Harpsichord. Composed by HENRY PURCELL, Composer in Ordinary to his most Sacred Majesty, and Organist of his Chapel Royal.' He dedicated these twelve sonatas to the King, and advertised in the London Gazette for subscribers to the four separate part-books, which could be purchased for the inclusive price of ten shillings by those who would 'repair to his house in St Ann's Lane beyond Westminster Abbey and receive their Books'. The opening sentence of the introduction to the 'Ingenuous Reader' says: 'Instead of an elaborate harangue on the beauty and the charms of Music (which, after all the learned Encomions that words can contrive, commends itself best by the performances of a skilful hand, and an angelical voice,) I shall say but a very few things by way of Preface, concerning the following Book, and its Author: for its Author, he has faithfully endeavoured a just imitation of the most famed Italian Masters; principally to bring the Seriousness and gravity of that Sort of Music into vogue and reputation among our Countrymen, whose humour, 'tis time now, should begin to loathe the levity and balladry of our neighbours: the attempt he confesses to be bold and daring, there being Pens and Artists of more eminent abilities, (much better qualified for the employment than his or himself) which he well hopes these his weak endeavours will in due time provoke and inflame to a more accurate undertaking.'

The 'neighbours' were the French, whose love of dance music was notorious (though they could be passionately serious in their 'symphonies'). The 'famed Italian Masters' included Vitali, whose music was already known in England. And we learn from Roger North's *Comparison between the Elder and Later Music* that one of the circumstances that occurred 'to convert the English Music to the Italian taste was the coming over of old Nicola Matteis: he was a sort of precursor who made way for what was to follow. [This was in about 1671] An accomplished musician, and I know no master fit to be named with Corelli but him: all his compositions are full of the most [skilful] harmony, and his fire exquisite. As a grateful legacy to the English nation, he left with them a general favour for the Italian manner of harmony, and after him the French way was wholly laid aside, and nothing in town had a relish without a spice of Italy. And the masters here began to imitate them, witness Mr H. Purcell in his noble set of sonatas'.

*   *   *

Until the middle of the seventeenth century the word *sonata* meant little more than 'sound-piece': it was a convenient name for distinguishing a work for several instruments from a *cantata*, 'song-piece', or a *toccata*, 'touch-piece' for keyboard. But in the second half of the century the name was used for two distinct forms of composition. One was the *sonata da chiesa*, or 'church sonata', which consisted of four contrasting sections – slow, quick, slow, quick. The other, the *sonata da camera*, or 'chamber sonata', was what we now call a Suite: it consisted of dance forms such as the Allemande, Couranto, Sarabande and Gigue. (The names for the two types were not meant to imply that dances were unsuitable for playing in church: Purcell's contemporary, the great Scandinavian composer Buxtehude, wrote organ Sarabandes and Gigues founded on well-known hymn tunes, which influenced Bach to use dance forms for several of the most solemn choruses in his Passion music.)

It was the *sonata da chiesa* that 'the famed Italian Masters' brought to England in Purcell's time. The four sections were called by the Italian words that described the speed at which the music was to move. These Italian terms were not yet familiar in England, and the Introduction to Purcell's 1683 sonatas informs 'the English Practitioner' that 'he will find a few terms of Art perhaps unusual to him, the chief of which are the following: *Adagio* and *Grave*, which import nothing but a very slow movement: *Presto Largo, Poco Largo,* or *Largo* by itself, a middle movement: *Allegro,* and *Vivace,* a very brisk, swift, or fast movement.' (It was owing to the Baroque *sonata da chiesa* that the words 'first movement' or 'second movement' came to be used in the later, classical sonata of Haydn and Mozart.)

*　　*　　*

Twentieth-century historians think that Purcell's Introduction to the 'ingenuous reader' was probably written for him by his publisher, John Playford. It is certainly true that few composers have the time to write essays about music, as they are too busy writing the music itself. And Playford was already a close friend: it would have been easy for Purcell to tell him the sort of thing he wanted said, and then to leave him to do the actual writing. But there is one sentence in the Introduction that sounds as if it must have been written by Purcell himself. It is in the final paragraph, where he adds 'his hearty wishes that his Book may fall into no other hands but theirs who carry Musical Souls about them'.

In the year when they were published, the *Sonatas of III parts* came into the hands of some of the best amateur

21

musicians in London. This was in the house of the Lord Keeper North, in what is now Great Queen Street. In Roger North's *Life* of his distinguished brother he tells us that the Lord Keeper played the bass viol 'most distinct and swift', and that 'he cared not for a set of masters to consort it with him [except] once, under Purcell's conduct.' And then North gives us a brief glimpse of what may well have been the first performance of the *Sonatas*, with his brother playing consort-bass. 'He caused the divine Purcell to bring his Italian-mannered compositions, and with him on his harpsichord, myself and another violin, we performed them more than once, of which Mr Purcell was not a little proud, nor was it a common thing for one of his dignity to be so entertained'.

It is a vivid description, but it is exasperating. If only North had resisted the temptation to boast about the Lord Keeper's condescension, and had told us instead about the composer's harpsichord playing! They must have played together for hours if they went through some of the sonatas more than once, and Purcell probably gave them invaluable hints about speeds and the balance of loud and soft.

Seventeenth-century composers used very few expression marks. An occasional 'play soft' or 'play loud' was the only written advice the performer was given. They had not yet got into the habit of indicating crescendos and diminuendos. But it would be a mistake to think that they wanted their music to sound all on one level. In one of Matthew Locke's compositions he indicates that a passage is to be 'louder by degrees'. And on another occasion he even orders that the music should be 'violent'. Purcell never marks anything to be played with violence, but a passionate expressiveness is implied in the music of many of his sonata movements, both in the 1683 set and in the *Sonatas of IV parts*, published in 1697, which contains the famous 'Golden Sonata.'

The change of title for the second set of sonatas is very

misleading: if they had been published before Purcell's death he would not have allowed them to be described as 'of IV parts'. For both sets are 'Trio Sonatas'. The 'three parts' are for two violins and continuo, but they needed four performers, because the continuo part sounded incomplete without a bass viol to sustain the single notes and a harpsichord to fill in an improved realization of the chords suggested by the figured bass. In the printed part-books the viol's part is not identical with the bass line for the harpsichord. Very often the viol has a rhythmical figure in repeated quavers while the harpsichord is content with crotchets for the foundation of its chords. And sometimes the viol is given scales in semiquavers while the harpsichord has minims to play. These passages in shorter notes were called 'divisions' in Purcell's time, and a book describing how they should be played was written by Christopher Simpson in the year of Purcell's birth. In this 'Division-Viol, or Art of Playing extempore to a Ground', Simpson explains that '*Division to a Ground* is the Breaking of the Bass', and he goes on to say: 'A *Ground*, or *Bass* (call it which you please) is [written] down in two several Papers; One for him who is to play the Ground upon a *Harpsichord;* the Other, for him that plays upon the *Viol*, who, having the said Ground before his eyes, plays such a variety of *Division* in Concordance thereto, as his skill and present invention do then suggest unto him'. This might suggest that there was no need for Purcell to write out the divisions in his viol parts. Simpson, however, goes on to explain that an excellent improvisation is 'a perfection that few attain to'. 'True it is', he says, 'that Invention is a gift of Nature, but he that hath it not in so high a measure as to play *extempore* to a *Ground*, may, notwithstanding, give both himself and hearers sufficient satisfaction in playing such Divisions as himself or others have made for that purpose.' And the rest of the book consists of practical examples of how to divide the slow notes of a bass part into runs or rhythmical patterns.

These written formulas were a kind of stock-in-trade that any Baroque musician could use whenever he liked. Seventeenth-century composers had none of the nineteenth century's dread of not being original; they had no desire for a desperate independence, but borrowed unashamedly from each other, as a matter of course. And the division formulas lasted until the middle of the eighteenth century: the famous opening of Bach's third Brandenburg concerto is nothing but a string of conventional divisions on the chord of G, though Bach, being a genius, was able to transform the notes into an unforgettable tune.

Purcell, like Bach, could take hold of a well-worn formula and turn it into a characteristically individual tune. He was at his happiest when dealing with the sort of Ground that is called *basso ostinato*, in which the same short musical sentence is obstinately repeated, over and over again. With breath-taking invention he was able to draw out an inexhaustible stream of variations on an *ostinato*, each one sounding inevitable in its expressive beauty.

*   *   *

We are not told what Charles II thought of the music his Composer in Ordinary had dedicated to him. We can take it for granted that he would have hated the earlier string fantasias, for Roger North tells us that he had 'an utter detestation of Fancies. He could not bear any music to which he could not keep the time'. It seems likely that he got most enjoyment from the music that was played to him during his meals. Seeing his twenty-four 'violins' dressed in all their finery, he must have felt that he was just as well provided as Louis XIV. He certainly imitated *le roi soleil* on all possible occasions. Evelyn, in his diary, says that the King 'brought in a politer way of living, which passed to luxury and intolerable expense'. He describes a banquet in Whitehall to all the Companions of the Order of the Garter:

The King sat on an elevated throne at the upper end at a table alone; the Knights at a table on the right hand, reaching all the length of the room; over against them a cupboard of rich gilded plate; at the lower end, the music [i.e., the twenty-four string players]; on the balusters above, wind-music, trumpets and kettle-drums. The King was served by the lords and pensioners, who brought up the dishes. About the middle of the dinner, the knights drank the King's health, then the King theirs, when the trumpets and music played and sounded. . . . The cheer was extraordinary; the room hung with the richest tapestry.

These tapestries were the newly woven Gobelins which showed 'incomparable imitations of Versailles, and other palaces of the French King, with huntings, figures and landscapes, exotic fowls, and all to the life rarely done'.

The Banqueting House, built by Inigo Jones, is all that remains of the vast Palace of Whitehall: the earlier buildings, including the chapel, were destroyed by fire three years after Purcell's death. We can still see the huge room where the banquets were held, for it is now used as the Royal United Services Museum. The high ceiling, painted by Rubens, is still as it was in Purcell's time, with its panels representing 'Peace and Plenty', 'Harmony and Happiness' and 'Wisdom overcoming Envy and Rebellion'. It was probably in this magnificent hall that some of Purcell's *Welcome Songs* were performed in honour of the Royal Family. One or two of them may have been sung and played as Water Music on the Thames, for there are descriptions of stately pageants on the river, 'with various inventions, music, and peals of ordnance, both from the vessels and the shore', with the royal party in 'an antique-shaped open vessel, covered with a canopy of cloth of gold, supported with high Corinthian pillars, wreathed with flowers, festoons and garlands.'

*   *   *

Purcell wrote as many as seventeen *Welcome Songs* and

25

Birthday Odes as part of his duties as Composer in Ordinary to the Royal Household. The titles of some of these songs seem puzzling at first sight. Why should it have been necessary to welcome the King with such exaggerated fervour 'on his return from Newmarket', when he had only been there to enjoy his favourite pastime of watching the horse races? But then, when we look into it further, we find rumours of a plot to assassinate him in Hertfordshire when he was on his way to or from the Newmarket races. The times were still difficult: there were conspiracies and threats of rebellion, and the King had to form a new regiment, called the 'Life Guards', for his own protection. Therefore the *Odes* that were written for the royal family usually had some reference to the alarms of rebel war and the god-like power of the victorious monarch. Unfortunately the verses were often stilted, and their patriotism seldom achieved anything beyond a flat-footed banality. But Purcell was a composer who could make a very little go a very long way. He had what his contemporaries called 'a genius for expressing the energy of English words'. He could get hold of a word and enjoy its rhythm and repeat it over and over again, adding new life to it and making it sound more and more important at each repetition. When he asks his chorus to sing 'Welcome, welcome, welcome home!', the music glows with an infectious enthusiasm; the rising quavers of the accompanying instruments carry the triumphant rhythm from each repetition to the next, and 'the King's return to Whitehall after his Summer's progress' becomes an epoch-making cause for rejoicing.

Purcell is never afraid of sounding obvious. In a later *Welcome Song*, when the poet says 'Tune all your strings to celebrate His so much wished return', he seizes hold of the words 'Tune all your strings', and sends his violins busily scraping their way across open E's and A's and D's and G's. Only the very greatest composers can afford to be as obvious as this.

The *Welcome Songs* and *Birthday Odes* are seldom performed today, as the words often have a seventeenth-century flavour that is now inappropriate. It would be utterly impossible for present-day singers to address a twentieth-century Queen as 'Awful Matron'! But the odes in honour of St Cecilia are sung by choral societies, year after year, for the praises of music's patron saint can never grow out-of-date.

The first of Purcell's odes for St Cecilia's Day was *Welcome to all the Pleasures*. It was written in 1683 and the published score tells us that it was 'a musical entertainment performed on November XXII, 1683, it being the festival of St Cecilia, a great Patroness of Music, whose Memory is annually honoured by a Public Feast, made on that day by the Masters and lovers of Music.' Purcell dedicated the work to 'the Gentlemen of the Musical Society', by way of gratitude for their 'kind Approbation'. The words of the ode, by Christopher Fishburn, are beautifully appropriate for a gathering of amateur musicians:

> Hail to this happy place that seems to be
> The ark of universal harmony!
>
> Here the deities approve
> The god of music and of love;
> All the talents they have lent you,
> All the blessings they have sent you,
> Pleas'd to see what they bestow
> Live and thrive so well below,
>
> While joys celestial their bright souls invade,
> To find what great improvement you have made . . .

This last line, if read aloud in a matter-of-fact tone of voice, might easily seem naive and patronising. But Purcell, as always, was able to transform a bare statement into a gloriously convincing tune, and the fortunate members of the Musical Society who sang and played in the first performance must surely have felt that they were getting better and better at music during each line of the *Ode*.

*   *   *

A few weeks after this first performance Purcell was appointed chief 'keeper, maker, repairer and tuner of all His Majesty's wind instruments' at a salary of £60 a year and expenses. He needed the money, which was worth much more in those days. But the work must have taken up a good deal of the precious time that might have been spent in composing. Ten years before this, when he was apprenticed as assistant keeper, the experience of having to look after so many different instruments would have been well worth while to a boy of fourteen. But now he was responsible for employing workmen and seeing about transport, as the new appointment included 'licence and authority to the said Henry Purcell to take up within the realm of England all such metals, wire, wainscot and other wood and things as shall be necessary. . . . And in His Majesty's name and upon reasonable and lawful prices, wages and hire to take up such workmen, artificers, labourers, work and store-houses, land and water-carriages and all other needful things . . . and to take up all timber, strings and feathers necessary.' The feathers were for the harpsichords. Each string was plucked by a quill, and each quill had to be carefully chosen from the primary wing or tail feathers of a raven or a crow. The 'land and water-carriages' must have given Purcell more trouble than anything else. When the King decided to stay two or three weeks at Newmarket for the races, eight of his musicians in ordinary went with him, taking their instruments. An entry in the records mentions 'removing His Majesty's instruments from London to Windsor and to Newmarket and delivering backwards and forwards'. There is a hint of plaintive resignation in that 'backwards and forwards': any twentieth-century music organizer who has had the anxious task of moving a harpsichord across two counties and getting it tuned in time for the rehearsal will know what Purcell had to put up with.

28

Organ tuning must also have taken up a great deal of his time, though it is to be hoped that he had several people to help him in the early stages of the work. We know that 'mechanics' were employed as well as musicians, for in one of Roger North's graphic descriptions he says 'one may observe, as I have done sitting by an operator at work, that in tuning two pipes to an octave there shall be first (when wholly discordant) an intolerable jar, and as the artist moves the plug to reduce the sound to a consonance, first it shall come to a distinguished beating very swift and chattering and so slower, and at length to a sort of wallowing of the sound, and at last fall into the consonance, as into a notch, and there flow with all the quiet and evenness imaginable. . . . Thus those artists judge of tuning . . . not by the sweetness or unity of sound, but by the not striving, beating, shaking or wallowing. And in that manner these mechanics, injudicious of true Music, shall tune more exactly than the nicest [i.e., most scrupulous] musician.'

*   *   *

In the following year, 1684, Purcell became involved in the famous 'Battle of the Organs'. A new organ was needed in the Temple Church, and the authorities asked each of the two leading organ builders, Bernard Smith and Renatus Harris, to make a superb new instrument so that they could choose which they preferred. When the new organs were finished, the Benchers of the Middle Temple were in favour of Smith, while the Inner Temple supported Harris. A public competition was arranged, so that 'the best Judges of Music' could help in the decision. Purcell and Blow played for Smith, and Harris's organ was played by Draghi, an Italian composer living in London. The rival supporters continued to argue among themselves, but in the end Smith's organ was chosen.

It was a small instrument by modern standards, but it contained some of the newly imported stops that were specially suited to the Baroque style of playing. The Middle Temple Benchers preferred it 'both for sweetness and fulness of sound, besides the extraordinary stops, quarter notes, and other Rarities.' These 'quarter notes' were divided keys which were useful in the days before equal temperament, as they gave alternative tunings for G sharp and A flat, and for D sharp and E flat. In the earlier music, scales had been tuned so that each interval could be represented by a simple ratio such as $2/1=$octave, $3/2=$fifth, $4/3=$fourth. This worked well enough in keys with few sharps or flats. But the Baroque composers were adventuring into more distant modulations, and they found that A flats and D sharps sounded out of tune. The divided notes, however, were not altogether successful. Roger North thought they had little to recommend them. 'Some experiments', he wrote, 'have been made by more additional pipes which they call Quarter Notes, to gain a perfection of tune; but over and besides the increase of charge and encumbrance of the fabric, they find it will not by any means be obtained exactly to answer all the scales as may be required.' But North had an unbounded admiration for Bernard Smith as an organ builder. One of his 'divine' organs stood in the great gallery of North's country house: he referred to it as 'an inexhaustible magazine' for gratifying his 'continual thirst after Harmony'.

* * *

Very little of Purcell's own organ music has survived, and it is possible that he improvised a great deal of the time when he was on duty as organist of Westminster Abbey and the Chapel Royal, as there was so much other music to be provided for the services. In 1685 Charles II died, and Purcell had extra responsibilities in preparing the music for James II's coronation in the Abbey. On the great day, the Westminster choir sang near the large organ, and a second organ was set up for the singers from the Chapel Royal, while the instrumentalists were placed in a separate gallery. Purcell's magnificent anthem, *My heart is inditing*, was performed by the 'consort of voices and instruments' at the end of the long ceremony. It must have sounded overwhelmingly impressive, with the two choirs singing 'With joy and gladness shall they be brought, and shall enter into the King's palace', and with the strings answering the triumphant dotted rhythms from the opposite side of the Abbey.

The vitality in Purcell's church music is inexhaustible. Although he worked day after day at the same order of services, and heard the same responses over and over again, his settings are never perfunctory. 'As it was in the beginning' becomes an exciting phrase as soon as he gets hold of it: nothing is taken for granted, and the singers are caught up into his enthusiasm when he asks for the emphatic repetition of the phrase 'and ever, and *ever*, and EVER shall be'. He had learnt from 'the famed Italian masters' that the chief aim of writing for voices was to imitate the idea of the words, and he went further than any other English composer in exploring 'that very great affinity betwixt Language and Music'.

*　　*　　*

It is not only in his church music that the words live their own lives in such a startling fashion. His 'imitations' are equally convincing in his secular songs for the stage. When his librettist offers him the word 'laugh', Purcell transforms it into a tune that is so like a real laugh that the singer has no choice in the matter, but is compelled to let it turn into 'ha-ha-ha-ha-*ha*!'

Purcell had been writing theatre music since 1680. He could hardly have avoided it, for in the seventeenth century musicians had to 'hang between the church and the playhouse, and equally incline to both', for they depended on both for a living. Charles II had encouraged

31

his 'Chapelmen' to take part in the plays at the Duke's Theatre in Dorset Garden, and had announced that it was his pleasure that 'any men or boys belonging to His Majesty's Chapel Royal that sing at His Royal Highness Theatre do remain in town all the week during His Majesty's absence from Whitehall; only on Saturdays to repair to Windsor and to return to London on Mondays.'

In 1685 Purcell was writing incidental music that included one of the so-called 'mad' songs which were very popular at this time. The dramatist Thomas D'Urfey has listed the various degrees of madness that the public expected to be given: there were songs that were 'sullenly mad, mirthfully mad, melancholy mad, fantastically mad, and stark mad'. Purcell, being a highly professional musician, was always ready to supply what was wanted. But although he followed the fashion, he was never conventional in his settings, and the music of some of his Mad Songs is as dramatic and expressive as anything he ever wrote.

In this same year he was writing popular rounds, or 'catches', for a publication called 'Catch that Catch can, or The Musical Companion'. This collection includes such well-known rounds as 'Fie nay, prithee John', and 'Under this stone'. It is astonishing to realize that it was owing to the popularity of these 'ale-house' songs that public concerts were first given in London. Until then, performances of music could only be heard in churches, or at court, or in the home. But 'the public Music-meetings' began in Purcell's time; the first was 'in a lane behind Paul's: some shopkeepers and foremen came weekly to sing in consort, and to hear, and enjoy ale and tobacco: their music was chiefly out of Playford's Catch Book.' The next attempt, North tells us, was 'a project of old Banister, who was a good violin and a theatrical composer. He opened an obscure room in a public house in Whitefriars [where the publishing office of *Punch* now stands]; filled it with tables and seats, and made a side box with curtains for the music.

The Banqueting House in the Palace of Whitehall, 1689

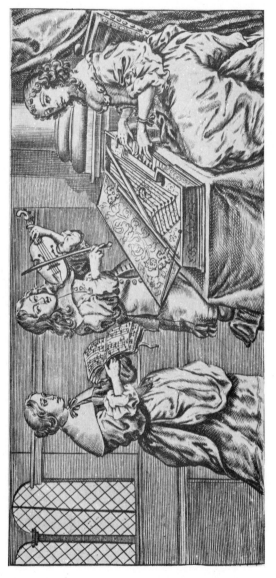

From the title-page of Playford's *The Banquet of Musick*, 1688, containing several songs by Purcell

One shilling was the price, call for what you please, pay the reckoning, and *Welcome Gentlemen*. There was very good music, for Banister found means to procure the best hands in town . . . and did wonders upon a flageolet to a through-bass. . . . The Masters of Music, finding that money was to be got this way, determined to take the business into their own hands; and it proceeded so far, that in York Buildings a fabric was reared and furnished on purpose for public music. It was called the Music Meeting, and all the Quality repaired to it.'

This was the first concert hall in London.

*   *   *

Purcell had no idea that his light-hearted catches were helping to make history. He wrote them, as he wrote his anthems and stage songs, because they happened to be needed. Although he was already popular as a composer, he was finding it difficult to earn enough to live on. The officials at Whitehall took their time about paying his salary as keeper of the organs, and in 1687 he had to send in a petition to the Treasury:

> The organ at present is so out of repair that to cleanse, tune and put it in good order will cost £40 and then to keep it so will cost £20 per an. at the least. . . . The salary of the place in the late King's time was £60 per an. for any care and trouble which will unavoidably occur. Wherefore I humbly pray that I may be established at the yearly salary of £56 to commence from Christmas 1687. And whereas it will cost to put the organ in repair as is above mentioned about £40, and my bill already delivered in, which ended at New Year's Day amounts to £20 . 10 . 0 since which the service performed amounts to about the like sum of £20 . 10 . 0, I humbly pray that order may be given for the present payment of the sum of eighty-one pounds.
>
> HEN. PURCELL.

This is the nearest approach to a letter from Purcell that has survived. He left no diaries or note-books, and it is only through his music that we can learn anything of his personal everyday life. When his friend and publisher, John Playford, died in 1686, we know what he felt about it when we hear his beautiful *Elegy on the Death of Mr John Playford*. Few music publishers can have had such a tribute as this lament for the 'good and friendly' business man whose life had been ruled 'by Harmony and Love'. Playford had done a great deal to encourage English composers during his thirty-five years as a publisher, supporting those who knew how 'to make English Words speak their true and genuine Sense', and having little patience with the snobbish gentry who chose 'to admire that in a Foreigner which they take little notice of in one of their own Nation'.

Fortunately for Purcell, John Playford's son Henry carried on with the publishing business, and in 1688 they were working together to bring out the first volume of *Harmonia Sacra, or Divine Hymns and Dialogues*, 'Composed by the Best Masters of the last and Present Age', with words 'by several Learned and Pious Persons'. Purcell made himself responsible for editing the works by composers who were no longer living, and the publisher's introduction assures the reader that 'his tender Regard for the Reputation of those great Men made him careful that nothing should be published which, through the negligence of transcribers, might reflect upon their Memory.' His own contributions to the two volumes of the *Harmonia Sacra* include some of the greatest music he ever wrote. These 'Divine Hymns' are not 'hymns' in our sense of the word. Many of them are full-length solo cantatas, with passionate declamations and brilliant runs and highly ornamented turns of phrase. The mood of the poems varies from the quiet exaltation of the *Evening Hymn*, 'Now that the sun', with its tirelessly repeated Alleluias, to the haunting desolation of 'In the black dismal Dungeon of

Despair, pin'd with tormenting Care; wrack'd with my Fears, drown'd in my Tears, with dreadful expectation of my Doom'. In the *Harmonia Sacra* Purcell had poems that were worthy of him, and he took hold of these vivid paraphrases from the Old and New Testaments and wrote settings that were far more dramatic than any of his songs for the theatre. *Saul and the Witch at Endor* is real 'drama in music': the imagined entrances and exits of the three characters are as clear to follow as they would have been if acted on a stage. And in *The Blessed Virgin's Expostulations* the singer's repeated cries of 'Gabriel!' on a clamorous high G are so compelling that listeners find themselves holding their breath in anxious suspense. Music such as this is 'operatic' in the true sense of the word.

*   *   *

In the same year that he was working on the first volume of the *Harmonia Sacra* Purcell was writing his great opera *Dido and Aeneas*. It is described as his only opera, because it is the only one of his many stage works where the music is continuous from the beginning to the end of the story. The songs and dances are not just strung together between long stretches of spoken dialogue: they are inseparably linked by recitative, which Purcell's contemporaries described as 'a kind of speaking in singing'.

There was nothing new about recitative. A hundred years before *Dido and Aeneas* the first inventors of opera had discovered that the characters in their dramas could converse in 'a kind of tuneful pronunciation, more musical than common speech, and less than song'. This discovery had taken place in a palace in Florence, where several poets, musicians and rich amateurs used to meet night after night to discuss their theories and carry out their experiments. They were not setting out to invent opera. All they wanted to do was to find out how the ancient Greeks had performed their tragedies, for they had been told that the words would have been sung in an expressive kind of chanting. The keenest of the rich amateurs advised the young Florentine composers to go to the theatre and to notice how the actors changed their speaking voices from high to low, and how each gesture and facial expression influenced the tone of voice. The young composers, Peri and Caccini, found that a good many Italian words were singable in ordinary speech, and they noticed that during a conversation an actor would pass through other words which were not so singable. They set these less singable words to music by letting the voice run through various quick syllables, while a *viola da gamba* held a long bass note that harmonized with the singable words. To add to the expressive quality of the sung recitation, a harpsichord player improvised a realization of the chords that were implied by each long-held note in the accompaniment. It was this invention of recitative that led to the birth of opera. Recitatives were used for representing action and for getting on with the story. Arias, which were 'the Songish Part', were intended 'to please the Hearing, rather than to gratify the understanding'.

* * *

Opera became immensely popular in Italy during the seventeenth century. In Venice alone there were eleven opera houses built between 1637 and 1679. It was in Venice that Evelyn heard and saw an opera for the first time: an entry in his diary during Ascension week of 1645 says:

> This night we went to the Opera where plays are represented in recitative music by the most excellent musicians, vocal and instrumental, with a variety of scenes, and machines for flying in the air. . . . Taken together it is one of the most magnificent and expensive diversions the wit of man can invent.

English audiences had not yet heard an opera in 1645, but they were familiar with 'machines for flying', owing to their elaborately staged masques, which were as expensive to produce as any Venetian opera. The account books for 1634 prove that in Charles I's time a masque called *The Triumph of Peace* had cost as much as £20,000. And Charles II could be just as extravagant over details. At a masque in Whitehall in 1675 the royal 'violins' were dressed in cherry-coloured taffeta, sky rich taffeta and yellow taffeta, with silver trimmings, while four 'gytarrhs' wore white taffeta with broad gold trimming. In this same performance we are told that '57 yards of gold and silver lace' were needed for the six 'shepherds of the chorus'. These six singers were almost certainly chosen from the choirmen of the Chapel Royal, and it must have been a startling change for them, after the sober routine of Matins at 10 and Evensong at 4, to find themselves swathed from head to foot in a shimmering cloud of lace ruffles.

The 'machines for flying' were already used in the London theatres in Purcell's time. Inigo Jones had brought the newest Italian innovations to the English stage, so that transformation scenes were now possible. The new theatres were very different from the old playhouses that Shakespeare and Ben Johnson had known: the buildings were now roofed in, and the stages had footlights and a drop curtain. Pepys noticed the difference in 1667 when he remarked that the stage was 'more glorious than heretofore. Now, wax candles, and many of them; then, not above 3 lbs. of tallow; now, all things civil, no rudeness anywhere; then, as in a bear-garden; then, two or three fiddlers; now, nine or ten of the best: then, nothing but rushes upon the ground and everything else mean; now, all otherwise'. By 1674 the decorations were far more elaborate and costly: according to a description of the Duke's Theatre, 'the band of 24 violins with the Harpsichords and Theorbo's' were placed 'between the Pit and the Stage.' 'While the Overture is playing', we are told, 'the Curtain rises and discovers a new Frontispiece, joined to the great Pilasters, on each side of the Stage.

This Frontispiece is a Noble Arch, supported by large Wreathed Columns of the Corinthian Order; the wreathings of the Columns are beautified with Roses wound round them and several Cupids flying about them. On the Cornice, just over the Capitals, sits on either side a Figure, with a trumpet in one hand and a Palm in the other, representing Fame'.

With such elegant theatres as this, London was able to welcome a French company in 1686 for the first performance in England of Lully's opera *Cadmus et Hermione*. We can take it for granted that Purcell was there to hear it, for he borrowed an instrumental *Entrée* from it, which he used as a dance in one of his later works. He probably learnt a good deal from hearing Lully's opera, but he must have learnt still more from the performance of *Venus and Adonis* by his friend John Blow. Although Blow called his work 'A Masque for the Entertainment of the King' it is a true opera, for there is no spoken dialogue. The recitatives tell us all that we need to know about the characters, and the swift changes of mood lead skilfully from one scene to the next. It was performed privately at court, before Charles II and a select audience. Members of the public were not yet ready for an opera with continuous music: they preferred stage plays with 'Singing, Dancing and Machines interwoven with them'.

*   *   *

Purcell, being a practical composer for the theatre, might never have written his *Dido and Aeneas* if it had not been commissioned for a private performance by amateurs in a girls' boarding-school in Chelsea. The school was kept by Josias Priest, a dancing-master with a good deal of theatrical experience. Purcell's librettist, Nahum Tate, managed to include seventeen dances in the short opera, so that 'the young Gentlewomen' could have plenty of opportunity for showing their skill. No description of this private performance has survived: we can only guess that the part of Aeneas and the male voices in the chorus were sung by some of Purcell's friends from the Chapel Royal and Westminster Abbey. The costumes, 'to gratify the Fancies of the Nobility and Gentry', may have been as 'Exorbitantly Expensive' as usual, but it is not likely that there were any 'machines for flying'. The building was described as 'the great school-house', but there cannot have been as much space as in a theatre. Purcell limited his orchestra to a few string players and a harpsichord, managing to draw from them all that he needed, without the help of flutes, oboes, trumpets or drums.

From the very first bar of the overture, the music sets the scene for the whole tragedy. When the curtain goes up, and the actors begin singing, we can immediately recognize them as individual human beings, for Purcell was able to give his characters a musical personality that was far more subtle and distinctive than anything a spoken libretto could give them. When Belinda, who is Queen Dido's waiting-woman, turns to her and sings 'Shake the Cloud from off your Brow', we recognize, from her tune, that she is both kindly and competent. Dido's reply, 'Ah! Belinda, I am prest with Torment', tells us that she is deeply in love and that she already knows that fate is against her. She repeats her slow, sad statements over and over again, and, miraculously, the words sound more and more convincing every time she sings them, for Purcell chose to build his long-drawn-out aria on the foundation of a *basso ostinato*, which makes its expressive beauty accumulative. Dido's ladies-in-waiting try to reassure her by singing 'Fear no danger to ensue, The Hero loves as well as you'. The lilting rhythm of the tune disregards the ordinary verbal accents and transforms the lines into a dance that is poised as well as flowing.

If *Dido and Aeneas* had been written for a professional theatre, the first entry of the royal hero would probably have had all the splendour of a flourish of trumpets. But as there were no trumpets in the Chelsea boarding-school, Belinda manages to suggest the sound of a fanfare in the shape of her tune as she announces 'See, your Royal Guest appears!'

In his scene in the Witches' Cave, Purcell may well have been influenced by his friend Matthew Locke's *Macbeth*. Locke had learnt how to be ruthless with a libretto. There is a passage in his *Macbeth* which looks like nonsense on paper, but it is just what is wanted as a basis for the Witches' music:

Hecate	Now let's dance.
2nd Witch	Agreed.
3rd Witch	Agreed.
4th Witch	Agreed.
All	Agreed. Agreed.

Purcell treats his *Dido* libretto in the same kind of way. 'Ruin'd ere the set of sun? Tell us, how shall this be done?' asks the leading witch during the second scene, thereby supplying the Sorceress with a conventional cue for explaining the plot to the audience. But Purcell never lets go of the dramatic tension, and his characters sound impatient to know what is going to happen next:

1st Witch	Tell us!
2nd Witch	Tell us!
1st Witch	Tell us!
2nd Witch	Tell us!
Both	HOW shall this be done?

Throughout every scene of the opera we can recognize Purcell's 'genius for expressing the energy of English words'. When the witches sing 'Destruction's our delight', their vigorous enjoyment leads them to exaggerate each consonant, so that the words are bristling and crackling with the vehemence of the malignant spells they are working. When a thunderstorm threatens to interrupt the royal picnic, Belinda's warning, 'Haste, haste to town, haste, haste!' has such a sense of urgency behind it that she manages to empty the stage of Queen and courtiers in less than three-quarters of a minute.

But it is in the expressive moments that the music of *Dido and Aeneas* reaches its most memorable heights. In the famous 'Lament' at the end of the opera, the chromatic harmonies are as poignant as in any of the greatest of Bach's tragic arias. Purcell keeps the long lines of the flowing music within the strictly formal pattern of a ground bass, and yet Dido is able to sing her 'Remember me' with the natural rhythm of the spoken words. It is in keeping with her musical personality that she should remain utterly simple and direct at the climax of her tragedy. The aria is 'artificial' in the sense that it is 'made with skill', but Dido is the most human of queens, from her first note to her last.

*   *   *

Purcell never wrote another real opera after *Dido and Aeneas*. He has been blamed for this by many historians, but it was not his fault. He was a practical man of the theatre, and he could not afford to go on writing works for private performances. The general public had little use for 'plays whereof every word is sung'. And the newspapers were insisting that opera was all very well for 'other nations', but 'Experience hath taught us that [the] English will not relish that perpetual singing'. The only way that Purcell could earn his living as a stage composer was by writing music for the 'sort of plays which were called Operas but had been more properly styled Semi-operas, for they consisted of half Music, and half Drama'. Soon after the performance of *Dido and Aeneas* he was working on the music of *The Prophetess, or the History of Dioclesian*, an adaptation of a play by Beaumont and Fletcher 'with Alterations and Additions after the manner of an Opera'. It was performed at the Dorset Garden Theatre, which was the chief centre of operatic production in London during the last quarter of the seventeenth century. *Dioclesian* 'gratified the expectation of Court and City'. And well it might, for the machines and spectacles were as magnificent as could be desired. The stage directions tell us that 'while a symphony is playing, a machine descends, so large it fills all the space from the frontispiece of the stage to the further end of the house, and fixes itself by two ladders of clouds to the floor. In it are four several stages, representing the Palaces of the Gods and Goddesses. . . . The whole object is terminated with a glowing cloud, on which is a chair of state, all of gold, the Sun breaking through the cloud, and making a glory about it; as this descends, there rises from under the stage a pleasant prospect of a noble garden, consisting of fountains, and orange trees set in large vases. . . . The Dancers place themselves on every stage in the machine; the Singers range themselves about the stage'.

Dioclesian was such a success that Purcell decided to publish the full score. Unfortunately he can have made very little money out of it. In his 'Advertisement' he says: 'I have been very careful in the Examination of every Sheet, and hope the Whole will appear as Correct as any yet Extant. My desire to make it as cheap as possibly I could to the Subscribers prevailed with me so far above the consideration of my own Interest that I find too late the Subscription money will scarcely amount to the Expense of completing this Edition'. The Dedication in the printed score is signed with Purcell's name, but it was written for him by Dryden. It says: 'Music and Poetry have ever been acknowledged Sisters, which, walking hand in hand, support each other. As Poetry is the harmony of Words, so Music is that of Notes; and as Poetry is a Rise above Prose and Oratory, so is Music the exaltation of Poetry. Both of them may excel apart, but sure they are most excellent when they are joined, because nothing is then wanting to either of their Perfections'.

42

*   *   *

Dryden was so much impressed by Purcell's 'happy and judicious Performances' in *Dioclesian* that he asked him to set three songs in his play *Amphitryon*. In the preface to the printed text of the play Dryden says: 'What has been wanting on my Part has been abundantly supplied by the Excellent Composition of Mr Purcell, in whose Person we have at length found an Englishman equal with the best abroad.' In that same year Dryden asked Purcell to write the music for his patriotic semi-opera *King Arthur, or the British Worthy*, and we get a glimpse of the occasional difficulties in their collaboration when we read Dryden's introductory remarks. He begins with a handsome compliment to Purcell, saying: 'Music . . . has arrived to a greater Perfection in England than ever formerly, especially passing through the Artful [i.e., skilful] Hands of Mr Purcell'. Soon, however, he is saying: 'the Numbers [i.e., the metre] of Poetry and Vocal Music are sometimes so contrary that in many places I have been obliged to cramp my verses, and make them rugged to the Reader, that they may be harmonious to the Hearer. Of which I have no Reason to repent me, because these sorts of Entertainment are principally designed for the Ear and Eye, and therefore in Reason my Art, on this occasion, ought to be subservient to his'. It is fortunate for us that Purcell got his own way in their arguments, for *King Arthur* contains some of his very best music. The tune of 'Fairest Isle' is one of the happiest of all his lilting dance-songs, and the famous Chaconne, borrowed from an earlier *Welcome Song*, has so much of Purcell's own musical character in it that performers cannot help feeling they know him as a person, every time they play it. His own contemporaries were chiefly impressed by the dramatic Frost Scene, where the 'Cold Genius' sings 'Let me free-hee-heeze again', while the strings tremble on each note with a teeth-chattering shudder. The audiences of the 1690's had never heard

43

anything like 'that exquisite piece called the freezing piece of music'. As Roger North said: 'The Noble Purcell was a match for all sorts of designs in music. *Nothing came amiss to him.*'

* * *

Only a few months after the first performance of *King Arthur*, another semi-opera by Purcell was advertised in the newspapers. 'I must tell you', says the *Gentleman's Journal* in 1692, 'that we shall have speedily a New Opera, wherein something very surprising is promised us; *Mr Purcell* who joins to the Delicacy and beauty of the *Italian* way, the Graces and Gaiety of the *French*, composes the Music, as he hath done for the *Prophetess*, and the last Opera called *King Arthur*, which hath been played several times the last Month.'

The 'surprising' new work was *The Fairy Queen*, an anonymous adaptation of Shakespeare's *A Midsummer Night's Dream*. It was the most ambitious of all the semi-operas: five different masques for singing and dancing were introduced as interludes in the spoken acts of the play. The preface by the anonymous adapter says:

> 'Tis known to all who have been any considerable time in Italy or France how Operas are esteemed among them. . . . If therefore an Opera were established here, by the Favour of the Nobility and Gentry of England, I may modestly conclude it would be some advantage to London. . . . That a few private Persons should venture on so expensive a Work as an Opera, when none but Princes or States exhibit them abroad, I hope is no Dishonour to our Nation. And I dare affirm if we had half the Encouragement in England, that they have in other Countries, you might in a short time have as good Dancers in England as they have in France, though I despair of ever having as good Voices among us as they have in Italy. These are the two great things which Travellers say we are most deficient in.
>
> If this [i.e., *The Fairy Queen*] happens to please, we cannot reasonably propose to ourselves any great advantage,

44

considering the mighty Charge in setting it out, and the extraordinary expense that attends it every day 'tis represented. . . We hope the English are too generous not to encourage so great an enterprise.

The audience was encouraging: we are told that 'the Court and Town were wonderfully satisfied with it'. They thought it superior to *Dioclesian* and *King Arthur*, 'especially in Clothes for all the Singers and Dancers; Scenes, Machines, and Decorations.' But the account goes on to say that 'the Expenses in setting it out being so great, the Company got very little by it.'

It is no wonder that the expenses were so extraordinary, for the stage directions are elaborate enough to daunt any twentieth-century producer. In Act III, 'the Scene changes to a great Wood. . . . A River in the middle; two great Dragons make a Bridge over the River.' In Act IV 'the Scene changes to a Garden of Fountains . . . enriched with gilding, and adorned with Statues. . . . Rows of Marble Columns support many Walks which rise by Stairs to the top of the House; near the top, vast Quantities of Water break out of the Hills, and fall in mighty Cascades.' In Act V 'Juno appears in a Machine drawn by Peacocks. The Peacocks spread their Tails and fill the middle of the Theatre.' At the transformation, 'the Scene is suddenly Illuminated and discovers a transparent Prospect of a Chinese Garden, the Architecture, the Trees, the Plants, the Fruit, the Birds, the Beasts quite different to what we have in this part of the World. . . . Over it is a hanging Garden. . . . It is bounded on either side with pleasant Bowers, and numbers of strange Birds flying in the Air.'

There were those in the audience who were not so wonderfully satisfied with the elaborate settings, and who complained of 'decorated nonsense'. But the majority of the public were getting just what they wanted, while the performers had to put up with their losses. And, all the time, Purcell was providing the necessary magic in every note of his music. When his fairies sing 'Trip it, trip it in a ring', the sound is so sparkling that there is no need for them to be dressed in gold and silver. When Titania's attendants lull her to sleep with their 'Hush, no more, be silent all', the stage is filled with the mysterious shadows of night. And in the last act, Purcell's 'Hark, the echoing air a triumph sings' is far more triumphant than any suddenly illuminated change of scene.

* * *

This year of 1692 was one of the busiest, as well as one of the most successful in Purcell's short life. His setting of Nicholas Brady's *Hail, bright Cecilia* was performed that November at the festival in honour of St Cecilia. With an orchestra of recorders, oboes, trumpets, drums, strings and continuo he could enjoy every detail that the verses offered him, from 'the noble Organ' to 'the airy Violin' and 'the amorous Flute'. The ode was 'performed twice with universal applause', the audience being particularly impressed by the 'incredible Graces' in the counter-tenor solo, ' 'Tis Nature's voice'.

These particular graces, or ornaments, are written out in full, but in many seventeenth-century songs only the bare outline of the tune is given, because the performers were supposed to invent the graces for themselves. We do not know how Purcell taught his pupils the art of gracing. There is only one anecdote that has come down to us, which gives us an unforgettable view of Purcell at work with his fellow musicians. A boy singer called Jemmy Bowen was practising one of Purcell's songs, when some of the choirmen 'told him to grace and run a Division in such a Place. "O let him alone", said Mr Purcell, "he will grace it more naturally than you, or I, can teach him".'

All that we can know of Purcell as a teacher is from reading the twelfth edition of Playford's *Introduction to the Skill of Music*, which Purcell revised in 1694. In the section on *The Art of Descant, or composing Music in Parts* he gives

46

admirably clear and practical advice to the beginner. He begins with the statement that 'Music is an Art of expressing perfect Harmony, either by Voice or Instruments, which Harmony ariseth from well-taken Concords and Discords.' He then warns us that a discord must be 'placed between two Concords', and, having given an example of how to add a bass to a tune, he says: 'Now supposing there were no Bass to the Treble, try Note by Note which is the properest Chord to each'. And he goes through the whole tune, just as if his readers were in the same room with him. He gives practical reasons for everything he suggests, showing that he would have sympathised with those pupils who are continually wanting to ask 'Why?' He stresses the importance of having a good tune, saying that 'the Perfection of a Master' is to have 'a great deal of Art mixed with good Air'. His most valuable piece of advice is in his lesson on 'Divisions', where he says: 'There are also Dividing Grounds to Single Songs, or Songs of Two Parts, which to do neatly, requires considerable Pains, and the best way to be acquainted with them is to *Score much and choose the best Authors*'.

In all his remarks about composing, he shows his characteristic generosity to his fellow musicians. Even when disagreeing with Christopher Simpson he mentions that he admires his *Compendium* of 1667 as 'the most Ingenious Book' he has ever met with. And when he wants to give examples of canons, instead of quoting his own he says: 'There is a wonderful Variety of Canons in Mr Elway Bevin's Book, Published in the Year 1631, to which I refer the Younger Practitioners.' At the end of the book, after quoting a longer and more difficult canon, he says: 'This is a *Gloria Patri* of Dr Blow's, whose Character is sufficiently known by his Works; of which this very Instance is enough to Recommend him for One of the Greatest Masters in the World'.

*   *   *

47

Purcell's own Latin canons can be a perpetual joy to amateur singers in schools and village choirs, just as his incidental dances are an unending source of delight to amateur string orchestras. His incidental music for the theatre includes examples of the Saraband, the Jig, the Hornpipe and the recently invented Minuet, which had been Louis XIV's favourite dance. Purcell's own favourite was the Hornpipe, which was a dance in triple time with a syncopated rhythm: it was very different from the later 'Sailors'' Hornpipe. A Hornpipe from the first act of *Dioclesian* was published in Playford's *English Dancing Master* in 1695, with 'plain and easy rules' for dancing it. The steps and figures are not the same as they would have been on the stage in *Dioclesian*, for the Playford country dances were meant for social enjoyment. But the instructions give us a practical example of how Purcell's music was actually danced during the last year of his life.

He wrote incidental music for as many as nine plays during 1695. Although these works contain some of his finest music they are never revived as plays because the words are so poor. The songs and dances were seldom introduced as part of the story: the characters were content to interrupt the action, saying: 'Pray oblige us with the last new song'. Even some of Purcell's contemporaries were upset by this, and said that it was a disgrace that 'the finest music, purchased at such a vast Expense' should so often be 'thrown away upon the most miserable Poetry'.

*   *   *

One of the last plays that Purcell wrote the music for was *The Indian Queen*. The songs immediately became so popular that they were stolen by one of Playford's rival publishers and brought out in a pirated edition. It is almost too painful to imagine Purcell's state of mind when he came across one of these unauthorized copies and read the printed letter on the opening page:

The Publishers, to Mr Henry Purcell.

Sir,

Having had the good fortune to meet with the Score or original Draft of your Incomparable Essay of Music composed for the Play called *The Indian Queen*, it soon appeared that we had found a Jewel of very great Value; on which account we were unwilling that so rich a Treasure should any longer be buried in Oblivion, and that the Commonwealth of Music should be deprived of so considerable a Benefit. Indeed we well know your innate Modesty to be such as not to be easily prevailed upon to set forth anything in Print, much less to Patronize your own Work, although in some respects Inimitable. But in regard that (the Press being now open) anyone might print an imperfect Copy of these admirable Songs, or publish them in the nature of a Common Ballad, we were so much the more emboldened to make this Attempt, even without acquainting you with our Design; not doubting but your accustomed Candour and Generosity will induce you to pardon this Presumption. As for our parts, if you shall think fit to condescend so far, we shall always endeavour to approve ourselves

Your obedient servants

J. May,

J. Hudgebutt.

This is surely the most outrageous letter that any composer could be expected to put up with. There were no laws of copyright in those days. Performers could get a certain amount of protection through the seventeenth-century equivalent of our Musicians' Union, and lawbreakers could be 'apprehended for teaching, practising and executing music without the approbation or licence of the Marshall and Corporation of Music.' But there was no protection for a composer. And Messrs. May and Hudgebutt must have known perfectly well that Purcell had only recently published the full score of *Dioclesian* at his own expense, and that he had corrected the mistakes with his own hand. But even if Purcell had felt like protesting, it was almost too late. He had only a very short while to live, and the 'additional music' for the 1696 performance of *The Indian Queen* had to be written by his brother Daniel.

*   *   *

In November of 1695 he wrote a setting of 'From rosy bowers' in D'Urfey's *Don Quixote*. The printed edition of 1698 says: 'This was the last song that Mr Purcell set, it being in his Sickness'. In this song, which is one of the most dramatic pieces of music he ever wrote, there is a sudden change of mood at the words:

> Ah! 'tis in vain, 'tis all in vain,
> Death and despair must end the fatal pain;
> Cold despair, disguised like snow and rain
>   Falls on my breast.
> Bleak Winds in tempests blow,
> My veins all shiver and my fingers glow:
> My pulse beats a dead, dead march for lost repose,
> And to a solid lump of ice my poor, fond heart is froze.

He made his will on November 21. It says:

> In the Name of God, Amen. I, Henry Purcell, of the City of Westminster, Gentleman, being dangerously Ill as to the Constitution of my Body but in good and perfect Mind and Memory (thanks be to God) do by these presents publish and Declare this to be my last Will and Testament. And I do hereby Give and bequeath unto my Loving Wife Frances Purcell All my Estate both real and personal of what Nature and kind soever, to her and to her Assignees for Ever. And I do hereby Constitute and Appoint my said Loving Wife my sole executor of this my last Will and Testament, revoking all Former Will or Wills. Witness my Hand and seal this Twentieth First Day of November, Anno Dni. 1695 And in the seventh year of the Reign of King William the Third etc.
> H. Purcell.

It was the eve of the festival in honour of St Cecilia. Purcell, being 'in perfect mind and memory', may possibly have been able to give a thought to his friends in the Chapel

50

Royal who were involved in that festival. They were having to do without him in the singing of the psalm for the twenty-first evening of the month: 'Remember me, O Lord, according to the favour that thou bearest unto thy people: O visit me with thy salvation, that I may see the felicity of thy chosen'.

He died on that same day. He was buried in Westminster Abbey, and the music chosen for his funeral included his own anthem, *Thou knowest, Lord, the secrets of our hearts*, which he had composed for the funeral of Queen Mary II, eight months earlier. This was the anthem that impressed an ex-singer of the Chapel Royal so deeply that he still remembered it twenty years later as being 'rapturously fine and solemn, and heavenly in Operation, which drew tears from all; and yet a plain, Natural Composition, which shows the power of Music, when 'tis rightly fitted and Adapted to devotional purposes'. Seldom can a great composer have had such appropriate music at his funeral. For Purcell had not only composed the anthem and the dirge for trombones, but he had actually rehearsed the singers and players himself.

His tomb is at the foot of the organ. A tablet on a pillar near the grave says: 'Here lies Henry Purcell Esq., Who left this Life And is gone to that Blessed Place Where only his Harmony can be exceeded.'

*   *   *

A memorial volume of his songs, with the title *Orpheus Britannicus*, was published by Henry Playford in 1698. The first few pages are filled with pious poems written in his honour, describing his 'transcendent Genius' and saying that 'Sometimes a Hero in an Age appears, But scarce a Purcell in a Thousand Years'.

In his short life he had written sixty anthems, three services and a festival Te Deum, thirty-five sacred songs and hymns, a hundred and fifty secular songs and duets, twenty-five Welcome Songs and Odes, the incidental music for forty plays, his one true opera and five semi-operas, as well as twelve string fantasias, twenty-two sonatas for violins and continuo, and a number of dances for harpsichord.

His incidental theatre music was frequently performed during the ten or fifteen years after his death. But by the middle of the eighteenth century only the most popular of his tunes were kept alive. Handel's music had come to mean so much to English choral societies that they saw no reason why they need ever sing anything else. During the nineteenth century only a handful of people met regularly to sing and play Purcell's anthems and secular songs. Then, in 1876, the Purcell Society was founded 'for the purpose of doing justice to the memory of Henry Purcell . . . by the publication of his works, most of which exist only in manuscript'.

The founders of the society had set themselves a difficult task, for some of the most important manuscripts were missing. *The Fairy Queen* was lost in 1700: the Patentees of the Theatre Royal in Covent Garden offered twenty guineas reward for its return, but it was not found until two hundred years later. The lost manuscript of *Dido and Aeneas* has not yet been discovered: we have to make do with two inaccurate copies dating from the eighteenth century, one of which is in Worcestershire and the other in Tokyo. The Purcell Society editors, however, did the best they could with the available material, and a score of *Dido and Aeneas* was published in time for the bicentenary of Purcell's death in 1895, when a performance was given in London by the students of the Royal College of Music.

This performance helped to bring about a revolution in English music. At that time, young English song-writers were brought up almost entirely on nineteenth-century German opera, and they had never thought of expressing the energy of English words in their music. *Dido and Aeneas* was a revelation to them. Vaughan Williams and my father were among the students at that 1895 performance, and during the rest of their lives they spent a good deal of their time and energy in encouraging amateurs and professionals to sing and play Purcell.

English musicians of today have grown up with Purcell's music as a necessary part of their lives, and two of our greatest composers, Benjamin Britten and Michael Tippett, are continually acknowledging their immense debt to him in the actual music they write. In this way, Purcell's immortality is perpetually bearing new fruit. And that is as it should be, for he himself chose to be described as 'a real Friend and Servant to all Lovers of Music'.

INDEX

(Only the people and the subjects directly connected with Purcell are listed in this short index.)

Anthem, full 12
  verse 12

Banister, John (1630–79) 32
basso continuo 10
basso ostinato 24, 39
Birthday Odes 26
Blow, John (1649–1708) 6, 9

Canon 47
Catch 32
Chaconne 43
Chapel Royal,
  Choir School of the 5
  Gentlemen of the 3, 17, 37
Child, William (1606–97) 6
consort 15
Cooke, 'Captain' Henry (d. 1672) 5
counter-tenor 18
courtal 9

Dido and Aeneas 35, 38-41
Dioclesian 41
divisions 23
Dorset Garden Theatre 32, 41
Dryden, John (1631–1700) 5, 42
D'Urfey, Thomas (1653–1723) 32, 50

English Dancing Master, The 48

fancy, fantasia 16
Fairy Queen, The 44
flute 9
figured bass 10

Gostling, John (1650–1733) 19
gracing 46
Ground 23

Hail, bright Cecilia 46
Harmonia Sacra 34
harpsichord 22, 28
hoboy 9
hornpipe 48
Humphrey, Pelham (1647–74) 6, 7

Indian Queen, The 48
In Nomine 16

Jones, Inigo (1573–1652) 25

King Arthur 43

Locke, Matthew (1630–77) 13, 40
Lully, Jean Baptiste (1632–87) 7

Mace, Thomas (c. 1619–c. 1709) 6
Music Meetings 32
My heart is inditing 31

North, Roger (1653–1734) 20, 22, 29

Odes for St. Cecilia's Day 27, 46
'open notes' 9
organ 29, 33
Orpheus Britannicus 51

Pepys, Samuel (1633–1703) 4, 5, 13, 37
Playford, Henry (1657–1709) 34, 51
  John, (1623–86) 21, 34
Purcell, Daniel; brother (1660–1717) 50
  Frances; wife (d. 1706) 17, 50
  Henry, the elder; probably uncle (d. 1664) 3
  Thomas; probably father (d. 1682) 3

Purcell Society, The 52

'quarter notes' 30

recitative 35
recorder 9
regal 8
ritornello 12

sackbut 9
Simpson, Christopher (d. 1669)
16, 23, 47
Smith, Bernard (1630–1708) 29
Sonata 20
    da camera 20
    da chiesa 20
Sonata movements 21

spinet 9
Symphony 12

Tate, Nahum (1652–1715) 38
Thoroughbass (see *basso continuo*)
Thou Knowest, Lord 51
Trio Sonata 23
trumpet 9

Venus and Adonis 38
viol 15
viola da gamba 15
violin 13, 15
virginals 9

Welcome Songs 25, 52
Welcome to all the pleasures 27